TEA FOR FELICITY
A Play About Felicity
CHARACTERS

FELICITY
*A nine-year-old girl growing up just before
the American Revolution*

FATHER
*Felicity's father, a merchant who disagrees
with the king*

MISS MANDERLY
Felicity's teacher

ELIZABETH
*A shy nine-year-old girl from England,
who is Felicity's best friend*

ANNABELLE
Elizabeth's snobby older sister

ANGRY MAN
*A man who is angry at Felicity's father
for disagreeing with the king*

*The action takes place in the fall of 1774,
in Williamsburg, the capital of the
king's colony of Virginia.*

ACT ONE

Scene: Miss Manderly's parlor. Miss Manderly, Annabelle, and Elizabeth sit at the tea table.

(Felicity ENTERS.)

MISS MANDERLY: *(nodding and smiling at Felicity)* Good day, Miss Merriman. How lovely to meet you. I am Miss Manderly.

FELICITY: *(curtsies)* Good day, Miss Manderly. Thank you very much indeed for having me.

MISS MANDERLY: You are most welcome. Now I will introduce you to the other young ladies. They have just arrived in Virginia from England. This is Miss Annabelle Cole. And this is Miss Elizabeth Cole.

ANNABELLE: Oh, don't bother to call her Elizabeth. She's such a little bit of a thing, we call her *Bitsy* at home.

(*Elizabeth* looks unhappy.)

FELICITY: Good day, Annabelle. Good day…Elizabeth.

(*Elizabeth* smiles as *Felicity* sits at the tea table.)

ANNABELLE: (*snobbishly*) Your name is Merriman. You must be the shopkeeper's daughter. In England, Bitsy and I had our *own* governess. I never thought we'd have to share lessons with a shopkeeper's daughter.

FELICITY: (*proudly*) My father's store is the finest in Williamsburg!

MISS MANDERLY: (*firmly*) Young ladies. (*She pauses as all three girls bow their heads in embarrassment.*) Your parents have asked me to teach you the rules of polite behavior. Manners are observed most closely at tea. I will now instruct you in the proper way to serve tea.

ANNABELLE: (*rolling her eyes*) Good heavens! Bitsy and I know how to serve tea! We've watched Mama serve tea hundreds of times!

MISS MANDERLY: Splendid! Then you will be quite at ease, won't you?

(*Annabelle huffs.*)

MISS MANDERLY: Watch closely, ladies. I will ask each of you to serve the tea soon.

(*They watch as **Miss Manderly** gracefully opens the tea caddy, spoons tea leaves into the pot, pours water from the kettle onto the leaves, and gently swishes the pot to mix the water and tea together. She hands each girl a cup, saucer, and spoon and pours the tea as she says....*)

MISS MANDERLY: When the tea is ready, pour it very carefully. Offer your guest milk and sugar to put in her tea. Then offer her something to eat. (*picking up a plate*) Annabelle, would you care for a cake?

ANNABELLE: Oh, these are queen cakes! The Queen of England likes these. *(She greedily takes quite a few from the plate.)*

MISS MANDERLY: *(looking directly at Annabelle)* Remember, young ladies, you aren't eating because you're hungry or drinking because you're thirsty. *(to Felicity and Elizabeth)* The tea is offered to you as a sign of your hostess's hospitality. If you refuse tea, you are refusing her generosity.

FELICITY: *(sincerely)* Oh, I'd never refuse! You make the tea ceremony look so pretty.

MISS MANDERLY: Thank you, my dear. But you may not wish to drink tea all afternoon! There is, of course, a polite way to show that you do not wish to take more tea. Merely turn your cup upside down on your saucer and place your spoon across it. *(demonstrating)* And the correct phrase to say is, "Thank you. I shall take no tea."

FELICITY: Oh, dear…there is so much to remember!

MISS MANDERLY: Indeed, yes. A gentle-woman must know what to do in any situation. And now, young ladies, excuse me for a moment. All the queen cakes are gone. (*She picks up the empty plate and stands up.*)

(Miss Manderly EXITS.)

ANNABELLE: (*in a mean voice, as soon as Miss Manderly has left*) Well, of course, soon we won't have *any* tea to drink if these uncivilized colonists have their way.

FELICITY: (*puzzled*) What do you mean?

ANNABELLE: Haven't you heard? A few days ago in Yorktown, a mob of colonists threw chests of tea from an English ship into the river.

FELICITY: But why did they do that?

ANNABELLE: Because they are hotheads!
Simply a wild mob!

ELIZABETH: (*softly, to Felicity*) They didn't hurt
anybody.

ANNABELLE: (*glaring at Elizabeth*) Quiet, Bitsy!
(*to Felicity*) The colonists destroyed the tea
because they didn't want to pay the king's
tax on it. You colonists are *so* uncivilized.
You are ungrateful for all our king has
done. You…

(**Annabelle** *stops suddenly when* **Miss Manderly**
ENTERS with a plate of biscuits.)

MISS MANDERLY: Felicity, would you like a
biscuit?

FELICITY: Yes, thank you, ma'am.

*(**Felicity** bites the biscuit, then jumps up, hand to cheek, wailing.)*

FELICITY: Oooh! Ow!

*(**Annabelle** shrieks and jumps up onto her chair, as if afraid of a mouse. **Elizabeth** says "Oops!" as some of the silverware or silver pieces from the tea tray crash to the floor.)*

MISS MANDERLY: *(exclaims)* Ladies, ladies! Calm yourselves! Now! Miss Merriman, please tell us what happened.

FELICITY: I…well, it's my tooth…my loose tooth. It fell out when I bit into the biscuit and it…it fell into my tea! I'm so sorry, I…

ANNABELLE: *(wrinkling her nose in disgust)* Oh! How uncivilized! How rude!

MISS MANDERLY: *(kindly)* Don't fret, my dear. There was no harm done. I suppose a gentle-woman should know what to say in any situation. But I must admit, I don't know what to say when a tooth falls into the tea!

*(**Annabelle** scowls, but **Miss Manderly**, **Elizabeth**, and **Felicity** laugh happily.)*

ACT TWO

Scene: The Merrimans' store, two weeks later. Elizabeth is standing and looking on as Felicity sits in a chair carefully stitching her sampler.

ELIZABETH: Your sampler looks pretty, Felicity! We've been having lessons for only two weeks, and your stitchery has improved a lot!

FELICITY: I still don't like stitchery very much. But I do love our lessons at Miss Manderly's. *(smiles at Elizabeth)* Mostly I love them because of *you*. I'm glad you're my friend, Elizabeth.

ELIZABETH: I'm glad, too. *(plopping down in another chair)* Shall I tell you a secret? Annabelle is sweet on Ben. She thinks he's handsome!

FELICITY: Ben? My father's apprentice? Oh, that's too funny!

*(They giggle. **Father** ENTERS.)*

FATHER: Well, here are the two merriest girls in Virginia. *(He crosses to them.)* And what are you laughing about today?

FELICITY: Oh, we're just sharing a secret, Father.

*(Suddenly there is loud knocking at the door. The **Angry Man** ENTERS, waving a piece of paper that is a petition with many signatures.)*

ANGRY MAN: *(loudly)* Mr. Merriman! What is the meaning of this, sir?

*(**Elizabeth** and **Felicity** get up and back out of the way. They look worried.)*

FATHER: *(calmly)* Yes, I signed that agreement. More than four hundred other merchants signed it, too. We have decided not to sell tea anymore. It is our way of showing the king we disagree with his tax on tea.

ANGRY MAN: That is disloyal! It is wrong for colonists to go against the king! You know it is wrong, Merriman.

FATHER: (*firmly*) Sir! I have to do what I think is *right.*

ANGRY MAN: And what of those hotheads in Yorktown? Do you think they were right when they tossed good tea into the river?

FATHER: They threw that tea away to send a message to the king. They did what they thought was right.

*(**Elizabeth,** clearly upset by these words, EXITS by slipping quietly out the door.)*

*(**Felicity** is listening to the conversation and does not notice Elizabeth's departure.)*

ANGRY MAN: They were wrong to toss that tea! And you are wrong to stop selling tea. You are making a grave mistake. *(crossing to the door)* No Loyalist will ever shop in your store again! We won't give our business to a merchant who isn't loyal to the king.

FATHER: *(kindly)* Sir, you are my neighbor and my friend. Can't we disagree politely, without fighting? Fighting does no good.

ANGRY MAN: Humph! Good day to you, sir!

(**Angry Man** EXITS, *storming out.*)

FELICITY: *(sees Elizabeth is gone, runs to Father)* Father! That man frightened Elizabeth so much she ran away! Who was he?

FATHER: He is a Loyalist. He is angry because I've decided to stop selling tea in my store, to show the king we colonists will not pay his tax.

FELICITY: If no one pays the tax, it will make the king angry. Won't that start a fight?

FATHER: *(nodding his head sadly)* Aye. It could.

FELICITY: Do you think there will be a war?

FATHER: I hope not.

FELICITY: *(slowly)* Father, will we drink tea at home?

FATHER: No. There will be no tea in our house.

FELICITY: But what should I do at lessons? We drink tea there. *(pauses)* And teatime is so very important. What will Miss Manderly think if I refuse tea?

*(**Felicity** looks sad. **Father** hugs her.)*

ACT THREE

Scene: Miss Manderly's parlor, the next day. Felicity and Miss Manderly are standing by the table.

*(**Annabelle** and **Elizabeth** ENTER.)*

MISS MANDERLY: Ah, Annabelle and Elizabeth, good morning!

ANNABELLE and **ELIZABETH**: *(curtsying)* Good morning, Miss Manderly.

MISS MANDERLY: Elizabeth and Felicity, you may be seated. I'd like you to work on your samplers. *(They sit at the tea table.)* Annabelle, come with me please. We'll work on your handwriting.

ANNABELLE: *(snobbishly, as she hangs up her hat)* Good! It's so tiresome when I'm with Bitsy and that Merriman girl. My handwriting is so much better than theirs.

(Miss Manderly and Annabelle EXIT.)

(Felicity grins at Elizabeth and rolls her eyes about Annabelle. But Elizabeth looks down at her sampler and will not smile. With a mischievous look, Felicity gets up and puts on Annabelle's hat. She minces over to Elizabeth, batting her eyelashes and imitating Annabelle's voice, saying...)

FELICITY: Oh! Ben! It is I, your beautiful Bananabelle!

ELIZABETH: *(giggles)* Bananabelle? Oh, Annabelle...Bananabelle! *(looks toward the door nervously)* Do be careful, Lissie! If Annabelle saw you, she'd be angry. And she can be mean. I'm afraid of her.

FELICITY: *(in her own voice)* Oh, I am not afraid of Annabelle Bananabelle!

(Annabelle ENTERS and stands in the doorway scowling. Neither girl sees her.)

FELICITY: (*imitating Annabelle's voice and clasping her hands near her heart dramatically*) Oh, my darling Ben! Say that you love your Bananabelle! You know you have stolen my heart away! Let us be married! Oh, I love you, you handsome lad! Say that you will marry your Bananabelle, or I shall die!

ANNABELLE: (*outraged*) WHAT'S THIS?!

(**Felicity** *whirls around.* **Elizabeth** *gasps.*)

ANNABELLE: (*snatches hat*) Very amusing. So this is what you and your rude little shop-keeper friend do, Bitsy!

FELICITY: Oh, Annabelle! It was only a bit of fun.

ANNABELLE: (*angrily*) Fun? You have no manners! When Mama hears about this she'll tell Bitsy never to speak to you again! You horrible colonial brat! You…

*(**Annabelle** stops suddenly because **Miss Manderly** ENTERS and puts the tea tray on the table. **Annabelle** hangs up her hat, and then flounces over to her chair and sits.)*

MISS MANDERLY: Young ladies, the time has come for you to take turns serving the tea. Annabelle, you are the eldest. You shall serve the tea today.

*(**Annabelle** sits up very straight, acting important. **Felicity, Elizabeth**, and **Miss Manderly** sit down too. After **Annabelle** prepares the tea, she fills Miss Manderly's cup first, then Elizabeth's cup, and then her own.)*

MISS MANDERLY: Annabelle, my dear. You have forgotten to serve Miss Merriman.

ANNABELLE: *(smugly)* Oh! I was only thinking of the carpet.

MISS MANDERLY: The carpet?

ANNABELLE: Yes, indeed. I did not serve her because I did not want her to toss out the tea all over your fine carpet.

MISS MANDERLY: (*scolding*) Annabelle! Apologize at once!

ANNABELLE: Oh, but Felicity would be proud to toss out her tea. Her father said it is right to toss out tea. He said those hotheads in Yorktown were right to throw the tea into the river.

FELICITY: No! My father did not say that....

ANNABELLE: (*in a mean voice*) Yes, he did! Bitsy heard him in your store yesterday. Didn't you, Bitsy?

(*Elizabeth says nothing.*)

FELICITY: But that's not what he said! Tell her, Elizabeth!

*(**Elizabeth** won't look at Felicity.)*

FELICITY: My father said the men who threw the tea into the river *thought* they were right. They did it to show the king that they did not agree with the tax on tea.

ANNABELLE: Your *father* disagrees with the king's tax, too! That's why he's not going to sell tea in his store anymore. He is disloyal to the king. Your father is a traitor!

FELICITY: *(angrily)* No! My father is not a traitor! How can you say that? *(She turns to Elizabeth.)* How can you let her say such an awful thing, Elizabeth? You know it isn't true! My father is not a traitor— you are! You are a traitor to me!

> *(**Felicity** grabs her sampler and EXITS, running out of the room.)*

ACT FOUR

*Scene: The Merrimans' store, immediately after
Act Three.*

*(**Felicity** ENTERS, crying. She is carrying her
sampler. **Father** ENTERS.)*

FATHER: Felicity? *(worried)* What is it, child?
  What is the matter? *(He starts to cross the
  room toward her.)*

FELICITY: *(running to him)* Elizabeth and
  Annabelle think you are a traitor. I don't
  want to speak to them ever again!

FATHER: Ahhh. It's because of the argument
  about not selling tea in the store, isn't it?

FELICITY: Aye.

FATHER: My poor child. *(pauses)* I fear there is more of this trouble coming. This talk against the king will cause much sorrow before it is over. It will divide families and destroy friendships, if we let it. *(Gently, he takes Felicity's sampler from her hands.)*

FELICITY: Throw that sampler away! I hate it. It is full of mistakes.

FATHER: *(smoothing out the sampler)* There's a great deal that's good in this sampler. It would be a terrible waste to throw it away just because of a mistake or two. And I think it would be a terrible waste to throw away your friendship with Elizabeth just because of one misunderstanding.

FELICITY: She's not my friend! If she were my friend, she wouldn't have let Annabelle say such awful things!

FATHER: I see. You are afraid Elizabeth does not like you anymore. Is that it?

FELICITY: (*nods sadly*) Aye.

FATHER: I think you are wrong about that. But you will have to go back to your lessons to find out.

FELICITY: (*stubbornly*) I don't want to go to the lessons anymore! I want to forget everything I learned.

FATHER: Aye. (*holding up the sampler*) It is easiest to throw everything away. It is harder to untangle knots and try again. That takes courage.

FELICITY: (*slowly*) What if I do go back? What shall I do when they serve tea? I want to be loyal to you. I don't want to drink tea anymore. (*pause*) But if I am rude, Miss Manderly won't want me to come back ever again. Elizabeth won't want to be my friend. And Annabelle will think she is right, that colonists are uncivilized. (*Felicity looks at her father.*) What shall I do?

FATHER: Now that *is* a difficult knot to untangle. You must be polite, but do what you think is right. I trust you will find a way. (*smiling*) You have become quite a gracious young lady these past few weeks.

(***Father*** *kisses Felicity's forehead and EXITS.*)

ACT FIVE

Scene: Miss Manderly's parlor, the next day. Annabelle and Elizabeth are seated at the tea table working on their samplers as Miss Manderly looks on.

*(**Felicity** ENTERS.)*

MISS MANDERLY: Good day, Miss Merriman. I am very glad to see you today.

FELICITY: *(sitting down, taking out her sampler)* Thank you, Miss Manderly.

MISS MANDERLY: *(examining Felicity's work)* Why, Felicity, what fine work! You have untangled all the knots on your sampler.

ELIZABETH: *(bursts out)* Oh, Lissie! Annabelle twisted everything around. *(leaning toward Felicity)* I never said your father was a traitor. Annabelle said that, and I am so sorry I didn't stop her! I was afraid, but I won't be afraid anymore, I…

ANNABELLE: (*rises*) Bitsy! Stop that, Bitsy!

ELIZABETH: (*whirls around in her chair to face Annabelle*) I hate being called Bitsy! From now on, call me *Elizabeth*.

ANNABELLE: Why Bitsy, I…

ELIZABETH: Or I will call you Bananabelle in front of everyone. Annabelle Bananabelle.

(***Annabelle*** *huffs and sits down again, fiercely attacking her sampler to hide her anger.* ***Felicity*** *smiles at Elizabeth and squeezes her hand.*)

MISS MANDERLY: (*smiling*) Well, Elizabeth. Will you do us the honor of serving tea this afternoon?

(***Felicity, Elizabeth,*** *and* ***Annabelle*** *set aside their samplers.*)

ELIZABETH: Yes, indeed!

*(**Elizabeth** pours Miss Manderly's tea, then Annabelle's. Before she can fill Felicity's cup, **Felicity** takes a deep breath, and in a graceful gesture that the audience can clearly see, turns her teacup upside down on the saucer and puts her spoon across it.)*

FELICITY: *(politely)* Thank you, Elizabeth. I shall take no tea.

MISS MANDERLY: *(smiling)* Well done, Felicity! Very well done, indeed!

*(**Felicity** sighs with relief as she proudly takes a cake from the tray.)*